Eating Green & Loving It.

More than 100 **healthy** & **tasty** recipes.

By Dr. Duane Lund

Eating Green
& Loving It.
More than 100 healthy & tasty recipes.

First Printing 2011

Printed in the United States of America
by
Lund S&R Publications
Staples, Minnesota 56479

ISBN-13: 978-0-9740821-7-2
ISBN-10: 0-9740821-7-2

Dedication

To the members of the

Staples Table of Knowledge

that meets every morning

except Sundays and Holidays

at the local Burger King Restaurant.

Table of Contents

CHILLED SOUPS

CHAPTER III: Salads

CHAPTER IV:
Main Dishes and Side Dishes

CHAPTER V: Freshwater Fish

CHAPTER 1:
Entertainment Helpers

Hors d'oeuvres
Dips
Spreads
Sauces
Salsas

Food Substitutes

There are literally hundreds of no- or low-calorie substitutes available for dairy products, salad oils, cooking oils, spices, sugar, etc. Supermarket employees can help you locate them or you can check the Internet on your computer. A good place to start is on Google under "diet substitutes." You can then get more specific by checking topics such as, "dairy substitutes," "sugar substitutes," etc.

Once you have identified a specific product, be sure to check the label.

And, finally, if you have allergies or other health issues, consult your physician.

Toasted Almond Hors d'oeuvres

Ingredients to serve 6:

> **6 cups whole almonds, blanched (but may have skins on)**
> **2 T sugar or sugar substitute**
> **1t salt or salt substitute**
> **4 T extra-virgin olive oil or no- or low-calorie favorite oil**
> **2 t crushed red pepper flakes**

Combine the olive oil (or substitute) and red pepper flakes in a skillet and sauté over medium heat two or three minutes. Do not let boil. Stir constantly.

Transfer oil and pepper flakes to a bowl. Stir in the sugar and salt (or substitutes). Add the almonds and stir until well-coated.

Arrange the almonds on a flat baking pan, not touching. Bake in a preheated oven (medium) for 15 minutes—stirring a couple of times.

Marinated Olives Hors d'oeuvres

Ingredients to serve 6:

4 cups assorted olives, pitted (may be whole, halved, or sliced)
½ cup extra-virgin olive oil or substitute
Juice of one lemon
½ T pepper flakes, crushed
2 T fresh basil, chopped or torn into small pieces

Combine the olive oil (or substitute), lemon juice, and red pepper flakes in a skillet. Cook just briefly until the oil just starts to boil—only a minute or two—stirring all the while.

Remove from the stove and stir in the basil and olives, making sure they are all well-coated.

Let cool to room temperature and serve. (May be kept refrigerated a day or two in a sealed jar.)

Stuffed Celery Pieces

Use any variety of mushrooms.

Ingredients:

1 cup chopped mushrooms, fresh
3 oz. cream cheese or substitute
4 slices turkey bacon, broiled and crumbled
1 T onion, chopped fine
½ pound butter or substitute
1 bunch celery

Cut celery into 3- or 4-inch chunks. Sauté chopped mushrooms in butter until cooked through. Blend together all ingredients and stuff celery.

Mushrooms in Teriyaki Sauce

Ingredients:

4 cups halved fresh mushrooms or small whole mushrooms
1 cup teriyaki sauce
¼ pound butter or substitute

Sauté mushrooms in butter until tender. Add 1 cup teriyaki sauce and continue to heat (simmer) for 20–30 minutes. Drain mushrooms and serve hot, with sauce on the side for those who may want to dip mushrooms before eating.

Bruschetta Appetizer

Ingredients to serve 4:

4 slices Italian (or French) bread—a "generous" half-inch thick
1 large tomato, topped, seeded, and chopped (fairly fine)
2 T extra-virgin olive oil or your favorite substitute
3 T basil, torn or cut fine
1 clove garlic, minced
1/2 t each salt and pepper (or salt substitute)
mozzarella cheese, sliced thin, enough slices to cover bread (or cheese substitute)

Place bread slices on a baking sheet. Brush bread with olive oil. Combine all other ingredients except cheese. Ladle over bread slices; spread to cover each slice. Top each slice of bread with cheese.

Bake in a preheated 350 degree oven until cheese melts. (About 10 minutes.)

Cut each slice in half so that it is easier to handle.

Fresh Tomato Bruschetta (#2)

Ingredients to serve 4:

4 slices French or Italian bread, ½ inch thick
2 T virgin olive oil or light oil of your choosing
⅔ cup chopped tomatoes (cherry or larger)
3 T chopped basil
4 T shredded mozzarella cheese (or your favorite substitute)
4 green onions, chopped, both white and green parts

Brush bread slices with oil. Place under broiler until light brown.

Combine other ingredients and spoon over toasted bread slices. Cut each slice in half lengthwise.

Green Dipping Sauce

Ingredients to serve 6:

2 cups green olives with pimento stuffing
3 cloves garlic, minced
1 cup fresh parsley
2 ribs celery, chopped
1 cup mint leaves
juice of 1 lemon
½ cup cheese or cheese substitute of your choosing, shredded (Parmesan works well)

Using a food processor with a steel blade, blend until well mixed. Do not blend beyond the "chunky" stage.

A great dip for crackers, toast, vegetables, etc.

Sweet and Sour Sauce

Ingredients:

1 T green onion, white portion only, chopped
1 t garlic, minced
1 t ginger, minced
2 T low-calorie vegetable oil
1 cup water
1 chicken bouillon cube
¼ cup vinegar (preferably rice)
4 T sugar or substitute
2 T soy sauce
2 T cornstarch, dissolved in 2 T water

Sauté the onion, ginger and garlic briefly in the oil (about 2 minutes). Add all other ingredients and bring to a boil, then reduce to a simmer (do not let boil—just bubbly).

Stir in cornstarch-water mixture and continue cooking and stirring until it thickens to your preferred consistency.

Red Cocktail Sauce

Ingredients:

1 bottle chili sauce
1 pint jar tart jelly (currant, high-bush cranberry, etc.)
2 lemons, juiced
3 T horseradish

Combine all ingredients in a saucepan over low heat. Cook until jelly melts.

Serve hot with cocktail wieners or meatballs or cold with shrimp.

Pickle Relish Sauce

Ingredients:

1 cup light mayonnaise
3 T sweet pickle relish
1 t minced onion
½ t tarragon

Blend together all ingredients. Refrigerate.

Cucumber-Dill Sauce

Ingredients:

1 cup sour cream or substitute
1 medium cucumber (peeled, seeded, and chopped fine)
1 T minced dill
3 T light mayonnaise
1 T lemon juice
salt and pepper to taste

Blend all ingredients. Refrigerate.

Garlic Sauce

Ingredients:

2 T minced garlic
2 eggs (yolks only)
2 T lemon juice
1 cup olive oil or light oil of your choosing
1 t mustard
salt (or substitute) and pepper to taste

Combine all ingredients.

German Old-fashioned Cranberry Sauce*

Ingredients:

1 pound raw cranberries (you may use fresh or frozen)
2 large red apples with seeds and core removed
1 large orange with seeds and core removed (also cut off blossom end and bottom end)
2 cups sugar or substitute
1 cup water

Cut the cored and seeded apples and oranges into quarters or eighths. Run the cranberries and small pieces of apples and oranges through a hand food grinder. Instead of the hand grinder, you may use an electric food processor with a chopper attachment. Place the ground cranberries, apples, and oranges in a large saucepan

Add the sugar and water to the saucepan containing the ground cranberries, apples, and oranges.

Cook over low heat only until mixture is thickened and bright, clear red. Do not over-cook. Over cooking will make it very dark and bitter. Place in a large glass bowl. Serve with roast turkey, chicken or duck.

Recipe by Alice Altstatt; submitted by Lynn (Pappenfus) Durrenberger.

Oranges in Custard Sauce

Ingredients to serve 8:

10 navel oranges (remove peel and pith and cut into thin cross-sections)
1 cup sugar substitute
¾ cup water
¼ t lemon juice

Custard Sauce:
4 eggs, yolk only
¼ cup sugar substitute
4 T flour, all-purpose
1 cup milk substitute
1 t vanilla
2 T liqueur (maraschino if available)

Cut oranges and set aside. Make a syrup by boiling the sugar and lemon juice in the water. Boil until the sugar is dissolved and the liquid becomes syrupy.

Beat together the egg yolk and sugar; add flour; stir together. Meanwhile, heat milk to boiling point, but do not let boil. Add hot milk to egg mixture. Cook over low heat, stirring all the while until it thickens. Do not boil. Stir in the liqueur and vanilla.

Chill oranges and custard sauce for at least 8 hours. Pour custard over oranges when served.

Corn and Bean Salsa

Ingredients:

1 can whole kernel corn, drained
1 can black beans, drained
6 green chili peppers, chopped fine
3 medium tomatoes, diced
1 small onion, chopped
1 t garlic, minced
4 T vinegar

Combine all ingredients; mix well. Refrigerate 2 hours before serving.

Green Tomato Salsa

Ingredients:

3 large vine-ripened tomatoes, chopped*
4 green tomatoes (little or no red showing) chopped*
1 large onion, chopped
1 clove garlic, minced
½ t hot sauce (such as Tabasco)
1 T lemon or lime juice
½ t pepper

Skin and chop tomatoes. (They are easily skinned if immersed briefly in boiling water.) Combine all ingredients thoroughly, adding the hot sauce a drop or two at a time. Let stand, refrigerated, at least one hour.

*Chopped green and red tomatoes should be equal in volume.

Salsa with a Touch of Cumin

Ingredients for about 1 quart:

4 cups of mashed tomatoes (after they have been cored, cleaned, and skins removed.
To remove skins, place in boiling water a couple of minutes until skin wrinkles).
2 jalapeno peppers (Handle with kitchen gloves. Remove caps and chop very fine.)
3 T minced onion
1 T powdered cumin
2 T green pepper, chopped
2 T olive oil or substitute
2 T minced garlic
2 T vinegar
a "dash" of salt (less than 1 t) or substitute

Core, clean, skin, and mash the tomatoes. Chop the peppers, onion, and garlic.

Combine all ingredients. Let stand at least 1 hour before serving.

Garden Salsa

Ingredients:

12 vine-ripened tomatoes, peeled, seeded, and chopped
3 green (bell) peppers, seeded and chopped
2 jalapeno peppers, seeded and chopped (use rubber gloves)
2 medium onions, chopped
3 T vinegar
1 T sugar
1 t garlic salt

Place chopped tomatoes in a kettle. Bring to boiling, then reduce heat to simmer for about 15 minutes. Add all other ingredients and again bring to a boil. Reduce heat and let simmer 5 minutes. Extra salsa may be frozen.

Quick Salsa

Ingredients:

1 cup taco sauce (bottled)
2 large tomatoes, chopped
1 small onion, chopped fine

Combine all ingredients in a bowl. For a more zesty sauce, add a few drops of Tabasco or other hot sauce.

Peach (or Apricot) Salsa

Ingredients:

> **2 cups chopped peaches or apricots**
> **1 cup minced cucumber (first peel and seed)**
> **2 cups chili sauce**

Thoroughly combine all ingredients.

Chutney Fruit Salsa

Ingredients:

1 cup chutney of your choice
1 cup chopped honeydew melon meat
4 medium tomatoes, skinned and chopped
4 jalapeno peppers, chopped (use rubber gloves)
1 medium onion, chopped
2 T chopped cilantro
¼ salt or substitute
½ T pepper

Chop and thoroughly mix all ingredients.

Banana Salsa

Ingredients for 1½ cups:

1 large, ripe (but not over-ripe) banana, cut into small pieces
1 small green or red bell pepper, seeded and diced
2 T minced fresh mint
1 green onion (use white portion only) chopped
2 T lime juice (or lemon)
1½ T brown sugar or substitute

Combine all ingredients thoroughly.

Guacamole

Serve with hot chips as an hors d'oeuvres or as a side dish.

Ingredients for dip to serve 10:

4 avocados (or 3 large)
3T lemon juice, fresh
⅓ cup finely chopped scallions
⅓ cup finely chopped coriander
salt or substitute to taste

Cut each avocado in two: scoop flesh into a bowl. Mash with a fork. Add other ingredients, stir thoroughly and salt to taste.

Serve with hot tortilla chips.

CHAPTER II:
Soups

Food Substitutes

There are literally hundreds of no- or low-calorie substitutes available for dairy products, salad oils, cooking oils, spices, sugar, etc. Supermarket employees can help you locate them or you can check the Internet on your computer. A good place to start is on Google under "diet substitutes." You can then get more specific by checking topics such as, "dairy substitutes," "sugar substitutes," etc.

Once you have identified a specific product, be sure to check the label.

And, finally, if you have allergies or other health issues, consult your physician.

Tomato Basil Bread Soup

Ingredients to serve 4:

2–14½ oz. cans crushed tomatoes (preferably Italian style)
1 cup water
½ cup chopped basil
1 t oregano
3 slices Italian or French bread, one-inch thick, cut into 1 inch cubes, toasted
½ t each salt (or substitute) and pepper
2 cloves garlic, minced
4 T olive oil, divided (or substitute)

Brush bread slices with oil. Place under broiler until they turn brown. Cut into one inch cubes.

Sauté the minced garlic in the remaining oil for one minute or until it just starts to turn brown.

Meanwhile, combine the crushed tomatoes, basil, oregano, salt and pepper in a saucepan and bring to a boil. Reduce heat to low and stir in garlic and bread cubes.

(Flavored croutons may be substituted for the bread or combined with it.)

Zucchini Soup

Ingredients to serve 6:

2 pounds zucchini, peel two of the zucchini; chop these squash and remaining squash into quarter-inch chunks (save peelings)

4 cloves garlic, minced

1 onion, peeled and chopped

4 T extra-virgin olive oil or low-calorie oil of your choosing

5 cups water

½ cup basil, packed

½ t each salt (or substitute) and pepper

Sauté onion and garlic in the olive oil until onion is translucent. Add four cups of water, the chopped zucchini, and the salt and pepper and bring to a boil, then reduce heat to simmer and cook 15 minutes or until chunks are soft (stirring every few minutes).

Let cook, then purée the soup plus the basil in a blender in three batches. Meanwhile, cut the zucchini peelings into narrow strips and then cook these strips in the remaining cup of water until tender.

Re-heat soup until piping hot. Serve with strips of zucchini peelings floating on top of each bowl.

Minestrone (Vegetable Soup)

Ingredients to serve 6:

2 cloves garlic, minced
1 medium onion, chopped
2 ribs celery, sliced thin
4 T extra-virgin olive oil or low-calorie oil of your choosing
1 large (or two small) potato, peeled and chunked
1 carrot, scraped and sliced
1–14½ oz. can diced tomatoes (preferably Italian style)
1 medium zucchini, sliced
1 t basil, dried
1 t oregano, dried
½ t each salt (or substitute) and pepper
¼ t red pepper flakes
2 T catsup
5 cups water

Sauté the garlic*, celery, and onion in oil until onion is translucent.

Transfer to a soup kettle and add all other ingredients. Bring to a boil, reduce heat to simmer, and cook about 20 minutes or until vegetables are tender. Serve hot.

* Add garlic last; don't let it turn brown.

Carrot with Nuts Soup

Ingredients to serve 4:

8 medium carrots, scraped and chopped
⅛ pound butter substitute, melted or 4 T low-calorie oil
2 medium onions, peeled and chopped
1 t cumin
½ t pepper
4 cups water
3 chicken bouillon cubes
½ cup slivered almonds*, chopped
parsley for garnish

Sauté the onions and carrots in the melted butter for 3 to 4 minutes or until the onions are translucent.

Meanwhile, put the nuts under the broiler for a few minutes until they are crisp. Watch closely; do not let burn.

Add chicken broth and water to carrots and onions and bring to a boil; reduce heat; let simmer 15 minutes or until carrots are soft. Let cool. Mix together all ingredients and then purée in batches. Re-heat and serve hot. Garnish with parsley.

* May substitute walnuts or cashews.

Spicy Carrot Soup

Ingredients to serve 6:

10 medium carrots, scraped and sliced thin
⅛ pound butter substitute, melted, or 4 T low-calorie oil
2 large onions, peeled and sliced and broken into rings
3 cups water
2 chicken bouillon cubes
2 cups half and half or substitute
½ t nutmeg
½ t basil
1 bay leaf
¼ t Tabasco (or to taste)
chives, chopped, for garnish

In the melted butter, sauté the carrots and onion 3 or 4 minutes, stirring and tossing so that onions do not burn. Add all other ingredients. Bring to a boil, but do not let boil—reduce the heat at first indication it is about to boil. Simmer 15 minutes or until carrots are soft.

Garnish with chopped chives.

Beer Cheese Soup*

Ingredients to serve 4:

¼ pound butter substitute or 8 T low-calorie oil
½ t seasoned salt
¼ t celery salt
1 t Worcestershire sauce
½ cup diced onion
¼ cup diced celery
½ cup flour
2 cans condensed chicken broth or 2 cups water and 2 chicken bouillon cubes
1 can (12 oz.) beer
2 cups shredded cheddar cheese or substitute
popcorn for garnish (optional)

Melt butter in a large saucepan; add seasonings, onions, and celery. Cook over medium heat until vegetables are softened. Add flour, whisking to blend. Cook until bubbly; reduce heat to low and add remaining ingredients, whisking until cheese melts.

Garnish with popcorn (optional).

Courtesy (the late) Max Ruttger III, Gull Lake, Minnesota.

Cheesy Vegetable Soup

Ingredients to serve 4:

⅛ pound butter substitute or 4 T low-calorie oil
1 onion, peeled and chopped
2 medium carrots, scraped and chopped
2 celery ribs, chopped
2 medium potatoes, peeled and diced
1 green bell pepper, seeded and chopped
4 T flour
3½ cups water
2 cubes chicken bouillon
4 oz. cheddar cheese or substitute, grated or diced small
½ t cumin
½ t thyme
1 t pepper
chopped celery leaves for garnish

Sauté onions, celery, pepper and carrots 2 or 3 minutes until onion is translucent. Move to a soup pot. Add all ingredients. Sprinkle in flour and continue to heat and stir another 2 or 3 minutes.

Carrot Soup with Apple

Ingredients to serve 6:

8 carrots, sliced thin
2 hard apples, peeled, cored, and chopped
1 onion, peeled and chopped
1 clove garlic, minced
2 ribs celery, chopped
5 cups water
3 chicken bouillon cubes
⅛ pound butter substitute or 4 T low-calorie oil
2 bay leaves
⅛ t black pepper
parsley, in sprigs or chopped, for garnish

Sauté the carrots, apples, celery, onion, and garlic in the butter substitute or oil (about 3 minutes or until the onion is translucent). Transfer to a soup kettle. Add all other ingredients and bring to a boil. Reduce heat to simmer and cook 30 minutes or until carrots are tender. Let cool. Remove bay leaves. Purée in batches. Return to kettle and cook until piping hot.

Garnish with parsley.

Ruttger's Lentil Soup*

Ingredients to serve 10:

2 cups lentil beans, rinsed
2 t salt
4 cups water

Place in a covered saucepan, simmer over low heat until tender (1 1/2 hours).

Water will be mostly absorbed by the beans.

4 T low-calorie oil
2 t seasoned salt or substitute
2 carrots, minced
2 ribs celery, minced
2 medium potatoes, peeled and diced
1 medium onion, peeled and diced

Add oil to pan. Add salt. Add vegetables and sauté, tossing and stirring occasionally until softened. Add 8 cups water (if desired, 1 cup of liquid can be dry white wine or sherry). Add lentils, simmer 1 hour, stirring occasionally.

Courtesy (the late) Max Ruttger III, Gull Lake, Minnesota.

Onion and Garlic Soup

Ingredients to serve 8:

6 medium onions, peeled and sliced
6 heads garlic, peeled and cut into quarters
6 cups water
3 chicken bouillon cubes
½ cup white wine
½ t thyme
salt and pepper to taste
¼ pound grated cheese or cheese substitute of your choosing for garnish

Place garlic and onion pieces in a small baking dish. Cover with 1 cup of water and 1/2 cup wine. Bake 1 hour at 325 degrees.

Remove from oven and place onion, liquid, and garlic in a soup pot. Separate onion rings and garlic cloves with a fork. Add remaining water, bouillon cubes, and spices. Bring to a boil, then reduce to simmer for 1 hour.

Serve hot with grated cheese or cheese substitute on surface.

Split Pea Soup with Potatoes

Ingredients to serve 8:

4 T low-calorie oil
1 onion, peeled and chopped
2 ribs celery, chopped
2 carrots, chopped
1 pound dry split peas, rinsed
7 cups water
3 chicken bouillon cubes
2 medium potatoes, peeled and cubed
1 t tarragon
1 T poultry seasoning
salt (or salt substitute) and pepper to taste

Sauté the onion and celery in the oil a few minutes until onion is translucent. Combine all ingredients in a soup pot and simmer 1 ½ hours (or longer if vegetables are not tender).

Garnish with croutons.

Potato Soup with Beets

Ingredients to serve 6:

3 medium potatoes, peeled and cubed
3 medium beets, diced
1 medium onion, chopped
1 rib celery, chopped
3 cups water
2 chicken bouillon cubes
1 cup half and half or substitute
2 T flour
2 T low-calorie oil
1 T dried, crushed spices of our choosing. You might try basil, tarragon, and/or rosemary. Total spices: 1 T
Garnish with chopped chives

Sauté the onion and celery in oil until onion pieces are clear (2 or 3 minutes). Stir in flour. Combine onion and celery in a soup pot with the potatoes, beets, water, bouillon cubes, and spices. Bring to a boil, then reduce heat to simmer and cook covered for about 20 minutes or until potatoes are tender. Let cool until it can be safely handled.

Process or blend the mixture in batches until smooth. Return to the kettle. Add half and half or substitute. Re-heat, but do not boil. Garnish with chopped chives.

Puréed Fresh Green Pea Soup

Ingredients to serve 4–6:

4 T low-calorie oil
1 medium onion, chopped fine
4 cups shelled fresh (or frozen) peas
1 rib celery, chopped
3 cups water
2 chicken bouillon cubes
1 t tarragon
Salt and pepper to taste (or salt substitute)
Optional: 5 slices turkey bacon fried crisp and broken into small pieces for garnish

Sauté the onion and celery in the oil a few minutes until onion is translucent. Place all ingredients (except bacon) in a soup pot and simmer 5 or 6 minutes until peas are tender.

Purée soup (in batches if necessary) until smooth. Pour through a coarse sieve. Return to kettle and, using medium heat, cook until hot.

Garnish bowls with bacon bits or croutons.

Potato Soup with Tomatoes

Ingredients to serve 6–8:

5 medium potatoes, peeled and diced
3 cans Italian style tomatoes
1 onion, chopped
2 ribs celery, chopped
2 cloves garlic, minced
2 bay leaves
½ cup cream or substitute
½ t sage
½ t oregano
4 T low-calorie oil
3 T catsup
Enough water to cover potatoes, plus 4 cups
parsley or celery leaves for garnish

In the oil, sauté onion, celery, and garlic a few minutes until onion is translucent. In a soup pot, cover the chopped potatoes with water and cook (boil) until potatoes are soft. Discard water. Add all other ingredients (including 4 cups of water and liquid in cans of tomatoes) and bring to a boil. Reduce heat immediately and let simmer about 10 minutes. Remove bay leaves.

Garnish with parsley or celery leaves. Serve piping hot.

Potato Soup with Carrots and a Hint of Orange

Ingredients to serve 6:

2 large potatoes, peeled and diced
4 carrots, sliced thin
5 cups water
3 chicken bouillon cubes
1 orange (juice of and rind grated)
1 bay leaf
1 T brown sugar or substitute
1 cup cream substitute
1 t Tabasco sauce
salt and pepper

In a soup pot, combine the diced potatoes, sliced carrots, water, sugar, Tabasco, and bay leaf. Bring to a boil, then reduce heat to simmer and cook for 20 to 30 minutes or until vegetables are tender. Let cool to handle safely. Remove and discard bay leaf. Add the grated orange rind and juice. Purée the soup in batches; return to kettle. Add cream or cream substitute and re-heat until piping hot, but do not let boil. Season to taste.

Sweet Potato Soup

Ingredients to serve 6:

3 large sweet potatoes, peeled and quartered
1 carrot, scraped and sliced
1 rib celery, chopped
1 onion, chopped
1 can lima beans, drained
1 t garlic salt
1 T brown sugar or sugar substitute
1 t cinnamon
4 cups water
add pepper to taste
parsley for garnish

Combine all ingredients in a soup pot. Bring to a boil, then reduce heat to simmer and cook for 40 minutes or until all vegetables are tender.

Option: Let cool and purée in batches and re-heat.

Add parsley for garnish.

Fresh Garden Tomato Soup

Ingredients to serve 4–6:

4 large tomatoes, peeled and diced
⅛ pound butter substitute or 4 T low-calorie oil
8 leeks, chopped, white part only
2 ribs celery, chopped
2 cloves garlic, minced
4 T tomato paste
4 cups water
2 chicken bouillon cubes
3 T catsup
6 drops Tabasco sauce
4 T chives, chopped for garnish (or parsley)

Sauté the onions, celery, and garlic a few minutes or until onion is translucent.

Combine all ingredients in a soup pot (except the garnish). Bring to a boil, then reduce heat to simmer and cook 20 minutes.

Garnish with chives or parsley.

...ado with Lime

...redients to serve 6:

3 avocados, pitted and peeled, cut into chunks
1 lime, juice only
5 cups chilled water
3 chicken bouillon cubes
1 t chili powder (level or rounded according to taste)
1 t powdered cumin
salt and pepper to taste (or salt substitute)

In a blender, place the chunks of avocado, lime juice, bouillon cubes, chilled water, cumin, chili powder, and salt and pepper. Blend in batches if necessary. Transfer to a bowl. Cover and chill 2 hours (longer than 3 hours may discolor the soup). If not cold enough, place in freezer compartment of refrigerator last 15 minutes. Soup may be garnished with a dollop of sour cream or low-fat garnish of your choosing.

Celery with Beets

Ingredients to serve 5–6:

4 ribs celery, chopped thin
3 cups water
2 chicken bouillon cubes
6 medium beets, peeled and diced
2 T sugar substitute
1 onion, minced
½ cup dry red wine
1 clove garlic, minced
3 t olive oil or low-calorie oil
salt and pepper to taste (or salt substitute)

Cook the celery, onion, and garlic in the oil until tender. Transfer to a soup pot. Add all other ingredients except the wine and cook over medium heat until beets are tender. Let cool. Add wine. Using a blender, purée in batches until smooth. Thin with ice water if consistency is too thick. Add salt and pepper if needed.

Chill several hours until very cold.

Peach with Yogurt

Ingredients to serve 5–6:

8 peaches, peeled, pitted, diced, and quick-frozen
2 cups orange juice, chilled
3 T sugar substitute
4 cups yogurt (blueberry, if available)
2 cups frozen blueberries

Stir the sugar substitute into the diced peaches.

In a blender, purée the peaches and orange juice. Do it in two batches, using half of each of the ingredients each time.

Combine with the yogurt.

Meanwhile, rinse the frozen berries (in a colander), just for a minute or two.

Serve the soup in bowls with the berries sprinkled on top.

Apple Soup

Ingredients to serve 8:

6 hard apples, cored and chopped
6 cups water
2 cinnamon sticks (about 8 inches in all)
1 T lemon juice
6 T sugar substitute
4 pieces cinnamon toast, crumbled
1 cup cream or milk or substitute

Place water, apples, cinnamon sticks, lemon juice, and sugar in a soup kettle.

Bring to a boil, reduce heat to simmer and cook 30 minutes or until apple pieces are soft. Let cool.

Discard cinnamon sticks.

In a blender, purée soup in batches. Strain through a sieve.

Refrigerate 4 hours or more (covered).

Serve in bowls over crumbled cinnamon toast. Top with cream or milk if desired.

Asparagus with Onion

Ingredients to serve 6:

2 pkgs. frozen asparagus, thawed and chopped (may substitute fresh)
2 large, sweet onions
¼ pound butter substitute (1 stick) or 6 T low-calorie oil
1 large potato, peeled and chopped
6 cups water
3 chicken bouillon cubes

½ cup dry white wine	½ t nutmeg
1 T thyme	1 T parsley flakes
1 cup yogurt	salt and pepper to taste
½ t marjoram	chopped chives for garnish

Sauté onions and asparagus in the butter substitute or oil for 4–5 minutes, stirring constantly so that onions do not burn. Transfer to a soup pot. Add all other ingredients except wine and yogurt. Salt and pepper to taste. Bring to a boil; reduce heat to simmer. Cook 30 minutes or until potato is tender. Remove from heat and let cool. Stir in wine. Add salt or pepper if necessary.

Using a slotted spoon, set aside 2 cups of solids. Purée the balance in batches until smooth. Combine solids with puréed soup. If too thick, add ice water.

Refrigerate at least 5 hours. Stir in yogurt just before serving. Garnish with chives.

Cucumber Soup

Ingredients to serve 4–5:

3 medium cucumbers, peeled and sliced very thin
1 sweet onion, sliced and broken into rings
3 T salt substitute

Place the cucumber slices in a flat bowl or glass baking dish. Sprinkle with salt. Let sit 30 minutes. Rinse and drain.

Transfer cucumber slices to a bowl. Add all other ingredients. Stir together thoroughly. Chill at least 4 hours.

Chilled Tomato Soup

Ingredients to serve 4:

    2 T extra-virgin olive oil or low-calorie oil
    2 cloves garlic, minced
    4 t onion, chopped
    3 pounds tomatoes
    2 cups seasoned croutons
    ⅓ cup basil leaves, torn into small pieces
    2 T sugar substitute

Sauté the garlic and onions a couple of minutes or until onion is just translucent.

Combine all ingredients and use a food processor to make an "almost smooth" soup.

Refrigerate and chill several hours before serving.

Scandinavian Fruit Soup

Fruit soup may be served either at the start of the meal or as a dessert or even for breakfast.

Ingredients to serve 8:

2 quarts water
½ cup raisins
1 cup prunes, sliced
1 cup apricots, sliced (or peaches or other fruit)
juice of ½ orange
juice of ½ lemon
4 T sugar substitute
½ cup tapioca
½ t salt or substitute
1 stick cinnamon

Place the fruit in the water; bring to a boil and then reduce heat and let simmer about 20 minutes. Let cool. Add all other ingredients and cook until the tapioca is transparent. Serve hot or cold.

Fruit Soup #2

Ingredients to serve 6:

2 cups chopped rhubarb
1 cup sugar substitute
1 cup water
1 T grated ginger root
1 cantaloupe, peeled, seeded, and diced
1 honey-dew melon, peeled, seeded, and diced
1 cup orange juice
pepper (dash or two)
1 cup fruit (any) flavored yogurt lightly sprinkled with pepper

Place the rhubarb, sugar substitute, and water in a stainless steel or ceramic kettle. Bring to a boil, then reduce heat to simmer. Cook 1 hour or until rhubarb is very tender. Let cool.

Set aside half the rhubarb, melon meat, and orange juice.

Stir together the remaining ingredients, add a dash or two of pepper, and purée in small batches in a blender.

Combine the purée with the set-aside ingredients. Chill, covered, at least 4 hours.

Cantaloupe Soup

Ingredients to serve 6:

6 cups diced cantaloupe
1 can peach nectar (comes frozen; let thaw)
1 T ginger, grated
1 cup yogurt
3 T sugar substitute

Combine all the ingredients thoroughly. Purée in batches until smooth.

Refrigerate for at least 2 hours. Also chill soup bowls.

Garnish with a sprig of parsley.

CHAPTER III:
Salads

German Style Potato Salad #1

Ingredients to serve 6:

10 small to medium potatoes, sliced or diced
1 small onion, sliced and broken into rings
3 ribs celery, chopped
2 cups salad greens
1/2 cup walnuts, chopped
4 T olive oil or low-calorie oil
3 T poppy seeds
2 T lemon juice or cider vinegar
3 T apple juice or cider
1 clove garlic, minced
Optional: 6 slices turkey bacon, fried crisp and crumbled

Cook the sliced or diced potatoes in a covered saucepan for 20 minutes or until done. Refrigerate 30 minutes.

Fry bacon until crisp, cool and crumble.

Make a dressing of the last five ingredients. Place all other ingredients in a bowl and gently fold in the dressing until everything is coated. Bacon bits may be used as garnish or folded in the salad. Serve hot or cold.

German Style Potato Salad #2

Ingredients to serve 6:

10–12 small potatoes, sliced or diced
3 T low-calorie oil
1 medium onion, sliced and broken into rings
½ cup wine or cider vinegar
½ t salt substitute
¼ t pepper
3 t chopped parsley for garnish
Optional: 6 slices turkey bacon, fried crisp and crumbled

Using a saucepan, cover the sliced or diced potatoes with water, then cook covered 20 minutes or until done.

Sauté the onion in the oil a couple minutes or until the onion is clear.

Place everything in the skillet. Stir gently over low-medium heat until all ingredients are warm (do not let burn).

Garnish with parsley or stir into the salad.

Serve hot or cold.

# Broccoli-Cauliflower Salad

Ingredients to serve 4-6:

1 medium head of lettuce, torn into pieces
1 cup fresh broccoli pieces (bite-size florets)
1 cup fresh cauliflower pieces (bite-size florets)
4 T grated parmesan cheese or cheese substitute
1 cup light mayonnaise
1/2 cup catsup
2 cup seasoned croutons

Place the lettuce, cauliflower, broccoli, and grated cheese or substitute in a large bowl. Stir together the mayonnaise and catsup (or use any dressing of your choosing). Gently stir the dressing into the salad. Top with croutons.

Waldorf Salad

Ingredients to serve 4:

4 large leaves of lettuce (on which to serve the salad)
2 large apples, peeled, cored, and diced
1 pear or peach or orange, peeled and diced
1 cup seedless red and/or green grapes, halved
1/2 cup walnuts, chopped
1/2 cup light mayonnaise or fruit salad dressing
1/2 cup whipped cream or substitute

Gently toss all ingredients and serve on the lettuce leaves.

French Red and Black Salad

Ingredients to serve 6:

1 head of lettuce
1½ cups black olives, pitted and halved
2 cups tomato chunks
½ pound of fresh mushrooms, sliced
½ cup olive oil or low-calorie oil
½ cup vinegar
4 T grated parmesan cheese or cheese substitute
1 t minced garlic
3 T fresh, chopped basil (optional)

Line salad plates with lettuce leaves. Combine mushrooms, olives, and tomatoes, and toss gently. Place oil, vinegar, and spices in a closed jar and shake. Pour over salad and toss gently. Spoon onto plates of lettuce.

Old-Fashioned Coleslaw*

Ingredients to serve 6:

    1 medium head of cabbage, shredded
    1 medium or two small onions, chopped fine
    1 small green pepper (not essential), seeded and chopped

Dressing ingredients:
    ⅛ cup of sugar substitute
    1 t salt substitute
    1 cup salad dressing or mayonnaise (light)
    1/2 cup tarragon vinegar

Mix together the cabbage, onions, and green pepper (shredded or grated or chopped fine).

Blend the dressing ingredients together.

Combine vegetables and dressing. Refrigerate and serve chilled.

Courtesy Harriet Dent; Staples, Minnesota

Red Cabbage Salad*

Ingredients to serve 10:

1 medium head of red cabbage, shredded
1 medium onion, chopped
¼ cup canola oil
1 cup applesauce
¼ cup cider vinegar
1 T honey
½ t salt
¼ t pepper
2 T pineapple juice

In a large skillet, sauté cabbage and onion in oil for 5–8 minutes or until tender-crisp. Add the remaining ingredients. Bring to a boil.

Reduce heat, cover, and simmer for 25 minutes or until cabbage is tender.

Courtesy Beth Chandler; Waite Park, Minnesota

Cabbage Salad (White or Red)

2 cups shredded cabbage
2 T shredded horseradish
1 cup applesauce
2 T onion, minced

Combine ingredients and chill.

Cabbage Salad

Ingredients for 6 servings:

1 head lettuce
1 medium onion, separated into rings
6 T of your favorite salad herbs. Dill, parsley, chives, or basil are all possibilities
(chopped)
4 T wine vinegar (if available, otherwise white)
6 T olive oil or low-calorie oil
1 T sugar substitute

Rinse and shake lettuce. Tear leaves into a large bowl. Add onion rings and chopped herbs. Mix together with vinegar, oil, and sugar. Toss together salad and liquids just before serving. Invite guests to add freshly ground pepper to taste.

Sweet and Sour Coleslaw

Ingredients to serve 6–8:

1 large head of cabbage, shredded
2 carrots, shredded
1 onion, chopped fine
1 rib celery, chopped
1 cup sugar substitute
½ cup vinegar
½ cup light vegetable oil
½ t salt or substitute
½ t pepper

Combine the sugar, vinegar, and vegetable oil in a saucepan. Bring to a boil, stirring regularly. Let cool.

Combine all other ingredients. Stir in sugar-vinegar-oil mixture. Refrigerate and serve chilled.

🐖 Apple Coleslaw

Ingredients to serve 8:

6 cups shredded cabbage
3 apples, peeled, cored, and diced
1 cup green, seedless grapes (halved if you have time)
1 cup chopped sweet pickles
3 T chopped sweet onion
1 cup light mayonnaise or light coleslaw dressing
3 T sugar substitute
2 T vinegar
3 T chopped sweet onions

Combine the cabbage, apples, grapes, pickles, and onions in a large bowl. In a small bowl, combine the mayo, sugar, and vinegar. Stir the contents of the smaller bowl into the contents of the large bowl.

Spinach Salad with Strawberries

Use your favorite spinach salad recipe and just add the strawberries or use this one.

Ingredients to serve 4:

> 4 cups spinach leaves, torn
> 2 cups frozen strawberries, thawed (or fresh, halved)
> 3 T sugar substitute
> 1 T sesame seeds
> 3 T wine vinegar
> ¼ t garlic powder
> ⅓ cup low-calorie salad oil of your choosing

Combine the spinach leaves, strawberries, and sesame seeds. Shake together the oil, garlic powder, vinegar, and sugar.

Mix all ingredients together thoroughly and then distribute into the salad bowls.

# Beet Salad

Ingredients:

      3 medium pickled beets, chopped
      1 apple, peeled, cored, and diced
      2 potatoes, boiled, cooled, and chopped
      1 T chopped onion
      1 cup sour cream (light or substitute)
      1 T mustard (prepared)

Combine all ingredients and chill.

Tomato Salad

Ingredients to serve six:

6 tomatoes, topped, seeded, and cut into bite-size pieces
2 cucumbers, peeled, seeded, and cut into thin slices
1 sweet green pepper, seeded and cut into narrow strips
1 onion, peeled and chopped
3 cloves garlic, minced
1 cup black olives, halved or sliced
6 basil leaves, cut or torn into small pieces
3 T parsley, chopped (for garnish)
1 T olive oil or low-calorie oil

Ingredients for dressing:

1½ cup extra-virgin olive oil or low-calorie oil of your choosing
4 T wine (or substitute vinegar)
½ t each salt, pepper, and sugar (or substitutes)

Sauté the garlic briefly in 1 T oil, then combine with all the salad ingredients, except the parsley.

Shake the dressing ingredients in a tightly closed container, then toss vigorously with the other salad ingredients and top each serving with parsley.

Tomato Salad #2

Ingredients to serve 6:

juice of one lemon
½ cup extra-virgin olive oil or low-calorie oil of your choosing
salt and pepper (or salt substitute)
2 pounds of tomatoes (may be a variety) sliced or cut into bite-size wedges
8 fresh basil leaves, torn or cut thin
Optional: ½ pound sliced or shredded cheese substitute

Prepare a dressing by whisking together the lemon juice, oil, and ½ t salt substitute and ½ t pepper.

Arrange tomato pieces on a platter. Drizzle the dressing over all. sprinkle with basil leaves.

Tomato-Garden Vegetable Salad

Ingredients to serve 4:

1½ pounds of a variety of tomatoes (red, yellow, cherry-size, etc.), sliced or cut
   into wedges
2 medium carrots, scraped and sliced thin
2 ribs celery, sliced thin
½ cup grated cheese or cheese substitute
4 T extra-virgin olive oil or low-calorie oil of your choosing
4 T wine or wine vinegar of your choosing
4 T fresh parsley flakes
1/2 t each salt and pepper (or salt substitute)

Shake wine, oil (or other dressing), salt and pepper in a covered jar.

Distribute tomato slices or wedges, carrots, and celery on four plates. Drizzle wine-oil mixture over vegetables. Scatter cheese and parsley over each serving.

Panzanella (Bread and Vegetable Salad)

Ingredients to serve 6:

5 slices Italian or French bread, one-inch thick (but into one-inch cubes)
1 cup green beans, cut into 1½-inch lengths
1 cup asparagus, cut into 1½-inch lengths
1 cup zucchini, sliced thin
½ cup extra-virgin olive oil or low-calorie oil of your choosing
12 cherry tomatoes, sliced in half
3 cloves garlic, minced
1 sweet onion, sliced thin and broken into rings
½ cup green olives, pitted and sliced in two
½ cup black olives, pitted and sliced in two
basil leaves sliced into 12 strips
½ cup wine vinegar

Brush one side of bread slices and place under broiler until golden brown. Turn over and repeat. Let cool and cut into one-inch cubes.

Place remaining olive oil in a skillet and sauté the asparagus, green beans, and zucchini until soft. Add garlic for one additional minute, stirring all the while.

Place all ingredients in a large bowl and toss.

Crispy Salad

Ingredients to serve 4:

4 cups Italian or French bread cut into ½-inch cubes
1 rib celery, sliced thin
½ medium-size cucumber, seeded and sliced
½ cup green onion, sliced (including green portion)
1 carrot, sliced thin and cut into half-slices
⅛ cup black olives, pitted and sliced
⅛ cup green olives, pitted and sliced
½ cup parsley, cut into 2–3 inch pieces
½ cup extra-virgin olive oil or low-calorie oil of your choosing
⅛ cup red wine (optional)

Bake bread cubes in preheated 350 degree oven on a pan. Bake 20 minutes, stirring bread cubes several times until golden brown. Cool completely.

Combine all ingredients, topping with parsley.

# Fruit Salad

Ingredients to serve 6:

3 apples, peeled, cored, and diced
1 small (8 oz.) can pineapple with juice (or fresh if available), cut into bite-size chunks
2 oranges, peeled and sections cut into 2 or 3 parts
1 cup blueberries
1 cup seedless grapes, green and/or red, halved
⅓ cup lemon juice
⅓ cup orange juice
3 T sugar substitute
juice drained from pineapple can

Combine juices and sugar; stir until sugar is dissolved. Place fruit in a large bowl; sprinkle with the juices and gently stir. Use a slotted spoon in distributing salad into 6 bowls. Sprinkle remaining juice over each.

Pasta Fruit Salad

Ingredients to serve 8:

1- 16 oz. package of shell (or similar) pasta
1 cup orange juice
2 cups yogurt (plain)
2 small cans mandarin orange slices, drained
1 pear, cored, peeled, and diced
2 cups seedless grapes, halved
1 large or 2 small apples (hard variety), cored and diced
⅔ cup shelled walnuts, chopped
2 ribs celery, chopped coarse

Prepare the pasta; let cool. Combine all ingredients, tossing gently.

Plan-ahead Jello Salad

Ingredients to serve 8:

2 pkgs. strawberry Jello
2 cups boiling water
2 cups cold water
1 pkg. frozen strawberries, thawed
3 bananas, sliced
2 cups miniature marshmallows (low-calorie, if available)
1 pkg. cream cheese or substitute
1½ cups whipped cream or substitute

Dissolve Jello powder in boiling water in a bowl. Add cold water, bananas, and about 2/3 of the strawberries and marshmallows. Pour into a square or rectangular dish or pan (about 8"x10"), sprayed with non-stick spray. Refrigerate until firm. Spread softened cream cheese over contents of the pan. Layer on a generous portion of whipped cream substitute. Scatter the remaining strawberries on top and cut into serving size squares.

Plan-ahead Cranberry Salad

Ingredients to serve 6:

2 cups cranberries (frozen, fresh, or in sauce)
½ cup sugar or substitute
2 cups miniature marshmallows (low calorie, if available)
½ cup green seedless grapes, halved
½ cup walnuts, chopped
1 cup whipped cream or substitute
lettuce leaves

Chop cranberries in a blender. Stir in sugar or substitute and marshmallows. Refrigerate overnight (or at least 3 hours). Stir in grapes, nuts, and whipped cream substitute just before serving. Serve on a lettuce leaf.

Mandarin Orange Salad*

Ingredients to serve 4:

Enough lettuce or salad greens to serve 4.
Small can mandarin orange slices, drained
1 cup sliced almonds, sautéed in butter substitute until brown
1 cup extra-virgin olive oil or low-calorie oil of your choosing

Sauté almonds in butter substitute.

Gently toss together all ingredients.

Courtesy Betsy Hayenga; Waite Park, Minnesota.

Bell Pepper Salad

Ingredients to serve 4:

4 bell peppers, may be of assorted colors
½ cup olives, pitted, may be a combination of black and green. May be sliced.
4 T extra-virgin olive oil or low-calorie oil of your choosing
3 garlic cloves, minced
salt substitute and pepper (½ t each)
2 T chopped parsley
2 T torn basil leaves

Bake the peppers in a 300 degree oven on a baking sheet for 20 minutes, turning occasionally. When they are done, they will start to blister and turn brown. Let cool, then seed and cut into bite-size strips.

Combine all ingredients in a bowl and toss until well coated with olive oil. May serve at room temperature or after refrigeration.

Three-Bean Salad

Ingredients to serve 4 (main-dish servings):

3 cans (about 16 oz. each) assorted beans
4 ribs celery, sliced extra thin
1 carrot, scraped and sliced extra thin
3 green onions, sliced, both white and green parts
1 head lettuce
4 T extra-virgin olive oil or low-calorie oil of your choosing
juice of 1 lemon

Combine all ingredients except the lettuce. Make beds of lettuce leaves on four plates.
Distribute equal portions of the salad ingredients on the beds of lettuce.

Three-Bean Wild Rice Salad

1 #2 can green beans, drained
1 #2 can yellow beans, drained
1 can kidney beans, drained
1 cup cooked wild rice (see recipes for cooking wild rice on pages 139 and 140)
½ cup green pepper, chopped
½ cup onion, chopped
1 cup cider vinegar
1 T Worcestershire sauce
1 t barbecue sauce
½ cup low-calorie salad oil
¾ cup sugar substitute
1 t salt substitute
1 t pepper

Drain all three cans of beans and place them in a bowl. Stir in the green pepper and onion. Mix the oil, vinegar, and all other ingredients. Pour over beans and mix well. Refrigerate in a covered dish overnight.

Wild Rice Garden Salad

(see recipes for cooking wild rice on pages 139 and 140)

2 cups wild rice, precooked and chilled
6 green onions, chopped (stems and all)
2 beet pickles, chopped
3 eggs, hard-boiled and chopped
1 egg, hard-boiled and sliced for garnish
2 T ripe olives, sliced
2 T celery, chopped
2 T chopped green pepper

Toss together all ingredients and place individual servings on beds of garden lettuce. Serve with vinegar and low-calorie oil or salad dressing.

Stuffed Tomato Salad with Wild Rice

¾ cup wild rice
6 large tomatoes
2 T chopped celery
3 garden green onions, chopped, including stems
2 T chopped green pepper
1- 2 oz. jar pimientos
½ cup slivered almonds or water chestnuts
1 cup low-calorie salad dressing

Prepare the wild rice by any of the basic methods on pages 139 and 140. Chill.

Prepare the tomatoes by placing them stem side down and cutting almost through 3 times with a sharp knife, making 6 wedges. Spread wedges apart (gently) making a basket for the salad.

Combine all ingredients and stuff each tomato.

Glorified Wild Rice

Prepare the wild rice by any of the basic methods on pages 139 and 140.

> 2 cups wild rice, precooked
> 2 pkgs. strawberry Jello
> 4 cups hot water
> 1 medium can crushed pineapple
> 2 cups whipped cream (or substitute)
> 1 cup low-calorie marshmallow bits

Prepare Jello and set in refrigerator until it thickens.

Beat whipped cream and Jello together; stir in remaining ingredients.

Chill before serving.

Additional whipped cream may be used as a topping.

Stuffed Apples

4 large apples (preferably a hard variety)
your favorite low-calorie jam
3 eggs, separated
3 T sugar substitute
2 T ground nuts of your choice

Peel and core the apples. Stuff them with the jam.

Beat the egg yolks and sugar together. Beat the whites until stiff and add to the yolks.

Pour over apples and then sprinkle each apple with the ground nuts. Bake in a 400 degree oven for about 20 minutes.

CHAPTER IV:
Main Dishes and
Side Dishes

🍅 Vegetarian Hot Dish

Ingredients to serve 6:

3 large potatoes, peeled and chunked bite-size
1 medium cabbage (about 2#) cut into bite-size chunks (discard core and outer portions)
1 large parsnip, peeled and sliced thin
1 large turnip, peeled and sliced thin
1 large carrot, scraped and sliced thin
1 medium rutabaga, peeled and diced
1 large onion, peeled, sliced and broken into rings
4 T low-calorie oil
½ t salt or substitute
¼ t pepper
Optional: grated low-calorie cheese as garnish

Cover the potatoes, cabbage, carrot, rutabaga, turnip, and parsnip pieces with water in a saucepan and boil, covered, until the vegetables start to soften. Using a slotted spoon, remove the cabbage after 3 minutes, all or the vegetables except the potatoes after 5 minutes and remove the potatoes after 10 minutes.

Sauté the onion rings in a skillet in half of the low-calorie oil.

Place all of the ingredients in a lightly greased baking dish or pan. Season with salt and pepper as you stir them together. Bake in a preheated 350 degree oven covered, one hour.

Pasta with a Hot Sauce and a Touch of Brandy

Ingredients to serve 4:

1- 16 oz. pkg. of pasta of your choosing
2- 14½ oz cans crushed tomatoes (preferably Italian style)
4 T extra-virgin olive oil or low-calorie oil
2 onions (medium) chopped
3 cloves garlic, minced
1 rib celery, sliced very thin
6 basil leaves, torn or cut into thin strips
½ t each salt and pepper (or salt substitute)
⅔ cup brandy (room temperature), vodka also works well

Sauté the onion, garlic, and celery in olive oil until the onion is translucent.

Add the tomatoes, basil, salt, and pepper to the skillet and cook until piping hot.

Meanwhile, prepare the pasta according to directions on the package and drain. Divide into four portions. Add the brandy to the sauce and pour equally onto the portions of pasta.

Spaghetti Sauce without Meat #1

Ingredients to serve 4:

1 box or 16 oz. pkg. spaghetti
2- 14½ oz. cans diced or crushed tomatoes, preferably Italian style (or use fresh
    tomatoes)
3 garlic cloves, minced
3 stalks celery, sliced very thin
2 carrots, scraped and sliced very thin
3 T extra-virgin olive oil or low-calorie oil
salt and pepper, ½ t each (or salt substitute)
2 basil leaves, torn thin

In a skillet, sauté the onions, garlic, celery, and carrots until the onion is translucent (about 10 minutes). Add the basil. Sprinkle with the salt and pepper, stirring well.

Add the tomatoes and continue to cook until the sauce starts to thicken.

Meanwhile, prepare the spaghetti according to directions on the package and drain. Divide the spaghetti on four dinner plates and top with equal portions of the sauce.

Spaghetti Sauce without Meat #2

Ingredients to serve 4:

1 box or 16 oz. pkg. spaghetti or other favorite pasta
1 pound fresh tomatoes
4 T extra-virgin olive oil or low-calorie oil
3 garlic cloves, minced
1 onion, chopped fine
3 T mozzarella cheese, small cubes, about 1/3 inch (or cheese substitute)
3 T finely chopped parmesan cheese or substitute
4 T torn basil leaves
salt and pepper (or salt substitute)

Sauté the onion and garlic in the oil in a skillet.

Using a food processor, pulse the tomatoes, cheese, onion, garlic, and basil. Stir in the cheese or cheese substitute and about 1/2 t each of salt (or salt substitute) and pepper.

Meanwhile, prepare the pasta according to directions on the package and drain. Divide the spaghetti on four dinner plates and top with equal portions of the sauce.

Spaghetti Sauce #3 with Lots of Herbs

Ingredients to serve 4:

1- 16 oz. pkg. spaghetti or pasta of your choosing
3 T extra-virgin olive oil or low-calorie oil
3 cloves garlic, minced
3 T minced onion
3 pound fresh tomatoes, chopped fine (save the juice)
salt and pepper (or salt substitute)
your favorite herbs (lots of them)

Sauté the garlic and onion in the oil until the onion is translucent (a couple of minutes). Add the diced tomatoes and juice to the pan along with 1/2 t dash of salt and pepper. Cook until piping hot. Stir frequently. Meanwhile, prepare the pasta according to directions on the package and drain. Remove the sauce from the heat and stir in your favorite herbs. Possibilities:

1/3 cup torn basil leaves
1 T chopped rosemary leaves
1 T chopped sage leaves
2 T chopped parsley
You may also add 1/2 cup or more of grated cheese of your choice (parmesan works
   well or cheese substitute)

Divide the pasta on four dinner plates and top with equal portions of the sauce.

Meatless Spaghetti Sauce #4

Ingredients to serve 4:

1- 16 oz. box or pkg. of spaghetti or other favorite pasta
2- 14½ oz. cans crushed or diced tomatoes (preferably Italian)
3 cloves garlic, minced or run through a garlic press
½ cup pitted and sliced olives of your choice
2 T anchovy paste or chopped anchovies
½ t red pepper flakes
3 T extra-virgin olive oil or low-calorie oil
½ cup basil, sliced or chopped

Cook spaghetti according to directions on the box or package.

Sauté garlic, anchovy paste or chopped anchovies in the oil for three minutes. Add tomatoes and olives and continue cooking until hot.

Drain the spaghetti and add to the pot and gently stir until pasta is well coated. Serve on four plates. Sprinkle with basil.

Spaghetti Sauce with a Bite* #5

Ingredients:

    3 cans Hunts tomato sauce
    1 can tomato paste
    ¼ cup olive oil or low-calorie oil
    1 medium onion, chopped
    3 cloves garlic, chopped
    1 cup water
    3 large bay leaves
    4–5 shakes of oregano
    1 t crushed red pepper
    1 T sugar or substitute
    dash of pepper
    shot of red wine

Prepare pasta according to directions on the package.

Sauté the onions and garlic in the oil. Add remaining ingredients and simmer for one hour. Liberally sprinkle with Parmesan cheese or substitute and simmer for an additional hour. Use immediately or freeze for future use.

* Courtesy Beth Chandler; Waite Park, Minnesota

Pasta with Mushroom Sauce

Ingredients to serve 4:

1 pound pasta of your choosing
1 cup fresh mushrooms, sliced (may use drained mushrooms, ½ cup)
½ pound butter substitute
4 T chopped thyme
4 T chopped basil
8 green onions, chopped, both green and white parts
1 cup grated Parmesan cheese or cheese substitute
½ cup milk or milk substitute or sherbet
½ t each salt and pepper (or salt substitute)

Prepare pasta according to directions on the package.

Sauté chopped onions, mushrooms, salt, pepper, and herbs in the melted butter substitute until the onions are brown and tender. Add milk and continue to cook. Stir until well blended.

Drain pasta, add sauce and cheese or substitute and toss until well coated.

Quick and Easy Tomato Sauce

For use with one pound of your favorite pasta.

Ingredients:

8 average size tomatoes, chopped
3 cloves garlic, minced
4 T extra-virgin olive oil or low-calorie oil
½ t each salt and pepper
herbs to be added—some or all, your choice:
6–10 basil leaves in strips, torn or chopped
3 t oregano
3 T parsley, chopped
2 T rosemary, chopped

Sauté the garlic in the oil for one minute, stirring all the while. Add the chopped tomatoes, salt, and pepper. Cook over medium heat, 10–12 minutes.

Stir in the herbs.

Penne Pasta with Tomatoes and Ripe Olives

Ingredients to serve 4:

1- 16 oz. pkg. or box penne pasta (or pasta of your choosing)
2 cans (14½ oz.) diced tomatoes (preferably Italian style)
3 T extra-virgin olive oil or low-calorie oil
⅔ cup ripe olives, pitted and sliced
3 cloves garlic, minced
2 T capers
10 basil leaves, torn or sliced thin
½ t red pepper flakes

In the oil, sauté the garlic a couple of minutes. Add the capers and continue another minute or two. Add the tomatoes, red pepper flakes, and olives and continue cooking until piping hot.

Meanwhile, prepare the pasta according to directions on the box and drain. Distribute the pasta on four plates and top with the sauce. Garnish with the basil.

Fresh Garden Peas, Green Onions, and Pasta

Ingredients to serve 4:

1 pound penne pasta or pasta of your choice
2 pounds fresh garden peas (no pods)
8 garden green onions, chopped, both green and white parts
4 garlic cloves, minced
4 T extra-virgin olive oil or low-calorie oil
½ t hot red pepper flakes
½ t each salt and pepper (or salt substitute)
1 cup grated cheese of your choosing (or cheese substitute)
1 cup water
juice of one lemon

Prepare the pasta according to the directions on the package.

Meanwhile sauté the garlic over low heat in the oil for just a couple of minutes. Add all other ingredients, but start with only a half cup of water and then add as much of the rest of the cup as needed to give you sauce that is not too watery.

Drain the pasta and divide among four plates and top with sauce.

Squash Side Dish

Ingredients to serve 4:

4 cups of sliced squash (One variety or two or three kinds. Zucchini blends well with many kinds of squash. If rind is heavy, remove before slicing. Cut thin slices or bite-size chunks.)

3 cloves garlic, minced

3 T extra-virgin olive oil or low-calorie oil

6 basil leaves, torn into small pieces

1 cup mozzarella cheese, grated (or cheese substitute)

In a heavy, non-stick skillet, sauté the squash pieces in the oil over medium heat for about 5 minutes or until squash is soft, stirring all the time. Add the garlic and stir for another minute.

Remove from heat and stir in basil and cheese. Serve hot. Have butter or substitute available as an option for your guests.

Orecchiette Pasta with Vegetables and Pine Nuts

Ingredients for 4 side dishes:

    8 oz. orecchiette pasta (funnel-shaped) or a pasta of your choosing
    1 cup broccoli florets
    1 cup asparagus, cut bite-size
    ½ cup pine nuts, toasted (or substitute a nut of your choosing, chopped)
    5 T extra-virgin olive oil or low-calorie oil
    3 cloves garlic, minced
    4 T Parmesan cheese, grated (or cheese substitute)

Dressing ingredients:
    ½ cup extra-virgin olive oil or low-calorie oil
    juice of one lemon
    1 t dill weed
    4 T wine or vinegar

Prepare the pasta according to directions on the package. Meanwhile, sauté the asparagus and broccoli in the oil until soft. Add minced garlic and stir for another minute.

Shake the dressing ingredients in a sealed jar. Toss with vegetables. Drain pasta and combine with vegetables. Toss some more. Divide into four warm bowls. Sprinkle each bowl with nuts.

Potatoes with Herbs on the Grill

Ingredients to serve 4:

Four potatoes, quartered (If large, cut into more sections. If skins are edible, leave them on.)
3 cloves garlic, minced
4 basil leaves, cut or torn into small pieces
4 thyme leaves, chopped fine
⅓ cup chopped parsley
½ t each salt and pepper (or salt substitute)
3 T extra-virgin olive oil or low-calorie oil

Combine the seasonings. Brush the potato sections with the olive oil. Roll sections in the bowl of seasonings.

Place potatoes between two sheets of heavy foil. Place on top of medium-hot grill. Cook for 20 minutes, then turn packet and cook for another ten minutes or until potatoes are tender.

Serve with leftover oil.

Spicy Spuds

Ingredients to serve 4:

4 large, red potatoes, skins on, cut into bite-size chunks (about 4 pounds)
½ cup extra-virgin olive oil or low-calorie oil
3 cloves garlic, minced
1 onion, minced
1 T (level) red pepper flakes (Adjust amount to how hot you want the potatoes.)
½ T salt or substitute

Combine the last four ingredients in a bowl. Brush the potato chunks with oil. Toss a few chunks at a time in the spices. Arrange potatoes on a greased cookie sheet—sides not touching.

Bake in a 350 degree oven for about 45 minutes or until potatoes can be easily pierced with a fork.

Drizzle leftover oil over potatoes before serving.

Seasoned Potatoes

Ingredients to serve 8:

4 large potatoes, sliced through lengthwise
2 T olive oil or low-calorie oil, divided into 2 portions
½ T Italian seasoning
¼ t salt or salt substitute
½ T pepper, freshly ground
½ t paprika

Make several half-inch cuts with a knife in the cut surface of each potato. Brush oil on the potato surfaces. Brush oil on a cookie or baking sheet. Place potatoes, cut side down, on the sheet. Bake 45 minutes at 350 degrees.

Mix 1 T oil with the seasonings. Turn potatoes over with a spatula and brush with seasoned oil. Return to oven, this time with cut side up, and bake another 45 minutes until done.

Boiled Potatoes with Dill

Use small new potatoes. Scrub clean. Cover with water, add a little salt and a few sprigs of fresh dill, and boil until done.

Serve with butter substitute or with milk (or milk substitute) seasoned with pepper and chopped chives as a gravy.

Swedish Brown Beans

1 pound dried brown beans
6 cups water
3 T vinegar (or 4 T catsup)
1 T salt or substitute
3 T syrup

Soak beans in water for 12 hours. Leaving beans in the water in which they have been soaking, add salt and bring to a boil. Cover, reduce heat, and let simmer 2½ hours. Stir in syrup and vinegar or catsup. Start with less, add more if it suits your taste. Small cubes of pork may be added during the boiling process.

Mashed Potatoes with Sweet Potatoes

Ingredients to serve 4:

3 large potatoes, peeled and quartered
1 large sweet potato, peeled and quartered
½ stick butter or butter substitute, melted
½ cup half and half or substitute
½ t salt or substitute
¼ t pepper
1 T brown sugar or substitute

Cover potatoes with water and boil for 15 minutes or until done—check with a fork.

Mash together all ingredients. use a hand masher or electric mixer.

Sweet Potatoes with Brandy and Nuts

Ingredients to serve 6:

2- 16 oz. cans sweet potatoes
4 T brandy*
1 cup pecans, crushed coarse
2 T brown sugar or sugar substitute
1/4 pound butter substitute, melted

Mash together all ingredients. Bake in a lightly greased, covered baking dish in a preheated medium oven for 25 minutes.

*May substitute bourbon

Sweet Potato Disks*

Peel and slice sweet potatoes into discs about 1-inch thick. Brush with olive oil or low-calorie oil. Place in a plastic bag with oil for a short time (turning over every so often). Place slices on a baking sheet. Sprinkle with salt and pepper or seasonings of choice. Bake in a preheated 400 degree oven for 20 minutes or until tender. Turn over once during baking.

*Courtesy Betsy Hayenga; Waite Park, Minnesota

Corn on the Cob

Remove the husks and silk and break off the stem. Rinse. Place the cobs in a deep kettle and cover with water. Add a couple of pinches each of salt (or salt substitute) and sugar.

Bring the water to a boil; let boil from three to five minutes (depending on the maturity of the kernels); let sit, covered, for a few minutes before serving with butter substitute. Let each season to his own taste.

Roasting Ears

Soak the ears of corn (husks and all) in water for at least 5 minutes. Wrap in foil and place in the embers of your campfire (or use your charcoal grill). Remove after an hour. Strip away the husks and silk (use hot pads or "mitts"), serve with salt and butter.

If you use the charcoal grill, you need not wrap the corn in foil. Just place them on the grill and turn every few minutes until the outside husks are singed.

Spicy Corn Chowder

Ingredients to serve 6:

3 cups whole kernel corn (from the can or frozen or cut fresh off the cob)
1½ cups water
1 chicken bouillon cube
1 cup cream substitute
3 Jalapeno peppers, seeded and chopped (use kitchen gloves)
   (or 1-4 oz. can chopped Jalapeno peppers)
1 sm. jar (2 oz.) pimentos, chopped

Purée half of the corn, peppers, and broth in a blender.

Combine all ingredients in a soup pot. Heat thoroughly, but do not boil.

Dandelion Greens

Ingredients to serve 6:

1 gallon dandelion greens (discard tough lower stems) cut with a scissors into
   2 to 3 inch pieces
3 cloves, garlic, mashed
⅓ t red pepper flakes
⅓ cup extra-virgin olive oil or low-calorie oil
½ t salt

Put greens in a large pot and cover with water. Sprinkle with 2 t salt; bring to a boil; cook 8 to 10 minutes or until greens are tender. Drain through a colander and rinse thoroughly with cold water.

In a skillet, add olive oil and warm over medium heat for 4 or 5 minutes. Add red pepper flakes and mashed garlic. Sauté until a light brown. Add greens and sprinkle with 1/2 t salt. Stir gently as you continue the cooking process for another 5 minutes or until greens are well covered with oil and other ingredients.

May be served hot or cold.

Vegetarian Casserole

Ingredients to serve 6:

3 large potatoes, peeled and chunked bite-size
1 medium cabbage (about 2 pounds) cut into bite-size chunks (discard core and
   outer portions)
1 large parsnip, peeled and sliced thin
1 large turnip, peeled and sliced thin
1 large carrot, scraped and sliced thin
1 medium rutabaga, peeled and diced
1 large onion, peeled, sliced, and broken into rings
½ stick butter substitute, melted, or 4 T low-calorie oil
½ t salt substitute
¼ t pepper
1½ cups cheddar cheese or substitute, grated or shredded

Cover the potatoes, cabbage, carrot, rutabaga, turnip, and parsnip pieces with water in a saucepan and boil, covered, until the vegetables start to soften. Using a slotted spoon, remove the cabbage after 3 minutes, all of the vegetables except the potatoes after 5 minutes and remove the potatoes after 10 minutes. Sauté the onion rings in a skillet in half of the butter substitute. Place all the ingredients, including the melted butter or substitute in a lightly greased baking dish or pan. Season with salt and pepper as you stir them together, but save 1/2 cup of grated cheese to sprinkle on top. Bake in a preheated 350 degree oven, covered, one hour.

Fried Green Tomatoes

Ingredients to serve 4:

6 green tomatoes sliced about a quarter-inch thick
3 eggs
½ cup water
⅔ cup cornmeal
½ cup flour
½ cup Parmesan cheese, grated (or cheese substitute)
½ cup extra-virgin olive oil or low-calorie oil
½ t oregano
1 T basil, chopped
1 t garlic salt
¼ t crushed red pepper flakes

Whisk together the eggs and water in a small bowl. Combine the cornmeal, flour, cheese, and seasonings in another bowl. Dip each tomato slice in the egg mixture and then in the second bowl.

Sauté the tomato slices in the oil, frying 4 or 5 minutes on each side until golden brown. Let dry on a paper towel, but serve them warm.

Ratatouille*

Ingredients to serve 6 as a side dish:

1 eggplant (about one pound), peeled and cut into bite-size cubes
1 or more zucchini (about one pound total), peeled and cut into bite-size cubes
4 T extra-virgin olive oil
3 large tomatoes, peeled, seeded, and chopped
2 red onions, sliced and broken into circles
2 red or green bell peppers, cut into thin strips about 2-inches long
3 cloves garlic, minced
½ t each salt and pepper
⅓ cup chopped basil
1 t thyme
1 bay leaf

In a large skillet, sauté the eggplant and zucchini pieces until tender (don't over-cook)—about 10 minutes. Remove eggplant and zucchini with a slotted spoon and set aside. In the same pan, reduce heat and sauté the onion rings two or three minutes, then add garlic and continue cooking another minute. Remove with a slotted spoon and set aside.

In the same pan, add the tomatoes and the remaining ingredients and cook another five minutes. Then return the set-asides to the skillet, cover, and continue to cook over medium heat another 10 minutes or until eggplant and zucchini are tender, but check every few minutes so as to not over-cook. Remove bay leaf before serving.

Courtesy Jerry Mevissen, Sebeka, Minnesota

Summer Vegetable Side Dish

Ingredients to serve 4:

Eggplant, 8 half-inch slices
Zucchini, 8 cross-cut half-inch slices
Tomatoes, 12 cherry-size tomatoes, halved or 3 medium tomatoes, quartered
2 cloves garlic, minced
1 onion, sweet variety, broken into rings
1 sweet green pepper, seeded and cut into strips
4 T extra virgin olive oil or low-calorie oil
4 T red wine
4 T flour
½ t each salt and pepper, combine with flour

Dust the eggplant and zucchini with flour and salt and pepper mixture and sauté (both sides) in the oil. (About six minutes per side.) Sauté the garlic along with the vegetables the last minute.

Optional: Sauté tomatoes along with the eggplant and zucchini in the last six minutes (or serve raw).

Divide the vegetables on four plates and scatter with onion rings and pepper strips and sprinkle with wine. Serve hot.

Zucchini with Wine

Ingredients to serve 4 as a side dish:

  4 large zucchini, sliced into half-inch sections
  4 T extra-virgin olive oil or low-calorie oil
  ½ cup red wine
  2 T chopped parsley

Sauté the zucchini in the oil in a large skillet. Brown sections on each side. Add wine and cook until wine evaporates, turning each section over once.

Sprinkle with parsley flakes as a garnish.

More Zucchini

Ingredients to serve 4:

3 medium zucchini, sliced cross-wise (should equal 3 to 4 cups)
2 cloves garlic, minced
1 medium onion, chopped
4 T extra-virgin olive oil or low-calorie oil
2 medium tomatoes, topped, seeded, and diced (not small)
1 T basil, torn or cut into small pieces
½ t oregano (dried)
1½ cups shredded cheese or substitute of your choice
½ t each salt and pepper (or salt substitute)

Saute the zucchini in the oil until soft. Add onion and garlic and continue a couple more minutes.

Add all other ingredients and continue cooking and stirring until cheese has melted. Serve hot.

Cabbage with other Vegetables

Ingredients to serve 8:

1 medium head cabbage, shredded
4 T low-calorie oil
3 medium onions, peeled, sliced, and broken into rings
6 cups water
3 chicken bouillon cubes
3 carrots, sliced thin
2 potatoes, peeled and diced
3 ribs celery, chopped
3 tomatoes, diced
1 t pepper
salt (or substitute) to taste

Sauté onions, carrots, celery. Transfer to soup pot. Add all other ingredients except cabbage and tomatoes. Bring to a boil then reduce heat to simmer; cook for 20 minutes. Add cabbage and continue to simmer another 10 minutes. Add tomatoes and continue to cook 10 minutes or until all vegetables are tender.

Red Cabbage (Rotkraut)

Ingredients to serve 6:

1 large red cabbage (about three pounds)
3 apples (medium to large) hard, red variety
1½ cups red vinegar (preferably wine vinegar)
1 T salt or substitute
6 cloves
2 cups water
1 T low-calorie oil
2 T sugar substitute
salt and pepper (or salt substitute)

Shred cabbage. Core and chop apples. Combine cabbage, apples, vinegar, salt, and cloves in a bowl. cover and let stand overnight. Add oil to a large kettle and heat. Pour cabbage mixture into the pot, then stir in the water and sugar. Simmer until tender. Season with salt and pepper to taste. Serve hot or cold.

"Doctored" Sauerkraut

Ingredients to serve 4:

2 cans sauerkraut (16 oz. each)
1 cup wine (preferably white)
½ cup brown sugar or substitute
1 onion, peeled and chopped
2 T low-calorie oil
1 hard apple, cored and chopped
1 potato (medium plus) peeled and chopped
4 cloves

Sauté the chopped onion in oil until brown. Drain the sauerkraut and add to the pot, sauté a few more minutes, stirring all the while. Add all other ingredients and simmer about 40 minutes. Serve hot or cold.

Baked Beans

(Doctored from the can. The Bush brand is my favorite.)

Ingredients to serve 4:

1 can (about 30 oz.) of pork and beans
2 pieces of turkey bacon, broken into bits
½ cup brown sugar (or ¼ cup molasses and ¼ cup brown sugar), or substitute
½ cup catsup
2 T mustard
a few pieces of green pepper
1 T chopped onion

Cut the bacon strips into half-inch pieces and fry over medium heat until brown, not crisp. Place the pieces of bacon and a little of the grease in the bottom of a kettle. (Help the dishwashers by using the same kettle for frying the bacon as you will use for heating the beans.) Add the beans, brown sugar, catsup, mustard, onion, and green pepper. Stir and heat (medium). Bring to a slow boil, then simmer for a few minutes. Stir occasionally.

Pumpkin and Squash (Dakota Sioux and Ojibwe Recipes)

Both were Native American foods and found wherever Indians chose to raise gardens. Early explorers brought the seeds from these plants back to Europe.

Indian cooks use at least three methods of preparation:

Method #1
Cut into chunks.
Leave skin on.
Scrape off seeds and stringy particles.
Bake by the fire on on the grill, turning for even cooking.

Method #2
Remove the skin and the seeds.
Cut into small pieces; place in pot.
Add a little water and maple sugar.
Cook over low heat until soft enough to be mashed.

Pumpkin and Squash (Dakota Sioux and Ojibwe Recipes)

Method #3
Cut off top (much as a child does when making a jack-o'-lantern).
Remove seeds.
Stuff with pre-cooked wild rice.
Add a little water to keep moist.
Place top back on.
Bake with low heat.

Potato Dumplings (Kartoffelklösse)

Ingredients to make 12 dumplings:

> **3 cups raw potatoes, peeled and grated**
> **3 cups mashed potatoes (use leftovers if you have them)**
> **4 T flour**
> **2 eggs**
> **1 T cornstarch**
> **1 t salt or substitute**

Mix together all ingredients. Meanwhile, start water boiling in a large soup kettle (about 3 quarts of water).

Make 1 dumpling—about the diameter of a half-dollar—and drop into the boiling water. If the dough starts to disintegrate, it means it is too soft. Add another tablespoon of cornstarch. Keep trying and adding cornstarch until the dumplings hold together. When it is the right consistency, make all the dough into half-dollar-size dumplings and drop them into the boiling water. Test after 5 minutes for doneness.

Rose Germann's Baseball Dumplings*

Ingredients to serve 6 as a side dish:

6 large potatoes, peeled, quartered, cooked, and mashed
4 slices toast (bite-size pieces)
2 cups flour
salt or substitute
1/4 pound butter or substitute, melted

Boil potatoes, mash, and let cool. Using hands, mix potatoes and toast. Mix flour with potatoes to form a ball about the size of a baseball. You may need more flour. Put balls in boiling salted water for 15 to 20 minutes. When they float to the top, use a slotted spoon to take out. Brown butter or substitute and pour over balls.

Sometimes Rose would use 1 or 2 eggs and 1 teaspoon baking powder

In memory of Rose Germann; Staples, Minnesota.

Rhubarb Dumplings

Make a dough of:

½ pound butter substitute, softened
3 T sugar substitute
1½ cups flour

Leave in a cool place for 20 minutes. Roll thin.

Make a filling of:

2 cups rhubarb, chopped
3 T sugar substitute

Cut dough into a half-dozen squares. Place rhubarb in center of each and sprinkle with sugar substitute. Fold the edges over the filling and press together. Bake in a hot oven.

Basic Preparation Recipes for Wild Rice

Method #1
1. Wash 1 cup wild rice
2. About eight hours before you serve it or use it in another recipe, place the rice in a saucepan or kettle and cover it with about 1 quart of boiling water.
3. About 30 minutes before serving or using in another recipe, drain and rinse.
4. Cover with hot tap water, add 2 teaspoons of salt, and let simmer until done.
5. Drain and fluff with a fork, adding salt and pepper to taste. If served as a side dish, add a pat of butter or substitute to each serving.

Method #2
1. Wash 1 cup rice.
2. Place in a saucepan or kettle and cover with 1 quart of water.
3. Add two level teaspoons salt or substitute.
4. Bring to a boil.
5. Turn down heat, cover, and let simmer until the rice is well "flowered."
6. Fluff with a fork; let simmer a few more minutes until done to taste.
7. Drain; add butter or substitute, salt and pepper; fluff once more.

Basic Preparation Recipes for Wild Rice

Method #3

1. Wash one cup wild rice; drain.
2. Place in saucepan or kettle, cover with water, and let stand overnight.
3. About 45 minutes before serving time (or using in another recipe), drain, and cover with 1 quart boiling water.
4. Add 2 level teaspoons salt or substitute
5. Heat until it starts to boil again, then lower heat and let simmer, covered, for about 40 minutes or until rice is done to your taste.
6. Drain, add butter or substitute, and fluff with a fork.

Method #4

1. Wash 1 cup wild rice.
2. Place in a saucepan and cover with 1 quart boiling water.
3. Let stand, uncovered, 20 minutes.
4. Drain and repeat three more times. The last time, add two level teaspoons of salt.
5. Drain, add butter or substitute, season to taste, and fluff with a fork.

⬤ Nutty Rice*

½ cup uncooked wild rice
2½ cups water
2 chicken bouillon cubes
1 small onion, chopped
4 T low-calorie oil
½ cup celery, chopped
½ cup chopped nuts (<u>not</u> finely chopped). Almonds, walnuts, hazelnuts, or cashews all
   work well, or even combinations.
Your favorite seasonings.

Wash rice.

Cover rice with two cups hot water and let stand overnight or about 8 hours before using. About
1 hour before serving time, drain and cover with chicken broth (made from 2 ½ cups of water
and the bouillon cubes). Bring to a boil, then reduce heat and let simmer for 30 minutes or until
rice is well flowered. (Better undercooked than overcooked at this point.)

Meanwhile, sauté the onions and celery in oil a few minutes or until the onion is clear.

Drain any excess liquid from the rice.

Continued on page 142

# Nutty Rice* continued

Place in a greased baking dish. Add onion, celery, and nuts. Lightly season with salt and pepper or your favorite seasonings, such a rosemary, thyme, parsley flakes, or marjoram. Stir together thoroughly.

Place covered dish in preheated oven (325 degrees) for 20 minutes, fluffing with a fork once or twice in the process.

*See chapter on Salads, pages 93 - 96 for more wild rice recipes.

CHAPTER V:
Fish

Fish

If you are having a tough time breaking your habit of making meat the centerpiece of the meal, switch to fish. It is probably the "greenest" of all meats and very enjoyable to eat.

Perch and Pineapple

Here's a Hawaiian treatment for Midwest fish:

1 pound perch fillets (or other freshwater fish)
½ cup pineapple juice
1 T lime juice
2 t Worcestershire sauce
½ t salt or salt substitute

Cut fish into serving-size portions. Place in a shallow baking dish. Combine pineapple juice, lime juice, Worcestershire sauce, salt, and a dash of pepper. Pour marinade over fish and marinate for 1 hour, turning once.

Drain, reserving marinade. Place fillets on a greased rack of a broiler pan. Broil 4 inches from heat until fish flakes. Brush occasionally with marinade. Heat remaining marinade and spoon over fish before serving.

Perch or other Small Fish with Parsley and Dill

This a turn-of-the-century favorite:

8 medium-sized perch, dressed (scale and remove heads, tails, entrails, and fins; and rinse)

Cover bottom baking dish with ¼ cup finely chopped parsley and arrange the fish in the baking dish.

Top with:
2 T finely chopped parsley
2 T chopped fresh dill or 1 t dill seed

Pour 1/4 cup hot water around the fish. Bake at 350 degrees for 20 to 25 minutes and serve. Whole crappies and sunfish also respond well to this treatment.

Poached Fish*

Here is a very different and exciting way to prepare fish.

Fillet the fish, remove skin, and cut into serving-size pieces about six-inches long. (The size doesn't really matter; you just want the pieces small enough to handle easily in the container you use for poaching.)

Fill a kettle about two-thirds full with cold water. Salt heavily (about one tablespoon per quart). Place the pieces of fish in the cold water.

Add two or three bay leaves or any other spices you prefer, such as whole black pepper or whole allspice. Add two tablespoons of vinegar—this helps kill house odors.

Bring to a boil gradually. When the water has attained a rolling boil, cut the heat back so the water just simmers. Allow the kettle to simmer for fifteen minutes or until the fish can be flaked with a fork. Be careful not to overcook; this will make the fish tough.

Remove the poached fish and place on a platter; drain. Flake the fillets with a fork into fairly large pieces (bite-size). Season with salt or substitute and pepper and brush the surface of each piece with melted butter or substitute.

The fish is now ready for serving, or you may try stirring the fish, seasoning, and butter together. Or instead of brushing the butter substitute on the fish, serve melted butter substitute on the side in a custard bowl or small dish and let your guests dip the fish as you would dip lobster.

*Courtesy the late Edward Morey, Motley, Minnesota

Poaching in a Frying Pan

This treatment is especially suitable for small, whole fish (all kinds); however, larger fillets may also be prepared in this manner. It is also a simple and convenient method of preparing fish over an open campfire.

If you plan to use the whole fish, the frying pan will need to be large enough to fit them in.

Clean the fish (remove head, tail, and fins, scale, and draw). Pour enough water into the frying pan to cover the fish. Add a dash each of salt, pepper, and celery salt. A bay leaf is also helpful, but optional. Slice an onion; break the slices into smaller pieces and place in the water. Bring to a boil (for 3 or 4 minutes), then reduce heat and submerge the whole fish in the liquid. Let simmer for about 10 or 12 minutes or until the meat can be easily flaked from around the exposed backbone at the large end of the fish.

Serve with lemon wedges.

Fillets from larger fish may be prepared in the same manner.

Poaching with Wine and Mushrooms

This recipe may be used with most any freshwater fish, but is especially good with walleyes, boneless northern fillets, or smallmouth bass.

Use a greased baking dish or oven pan, just large enough to accommodate—in a single layer—the amount of fish you wish to prepare.

Cover the bottom of the container with a layer of chopped mushrooms (pre-cooked or from the can).

Lay the fillets or small, whole dressed fish on the bed of mushrooms. Season lightly with salt and pepper. (If using whole fish, also season the inside of the body cavity.) For variety, you may want to try other seasonings, such as celery salt, parsley flakes, or onion salt. A few slices of onion would also add flavor.

Cover the fish with a solution of 2⁄3 water and 1⁄3 white wine.

Poach very slowly on top of the stove or cover dish or pan with foil (vented with a few holes to allow steam to escape), and place in a medium oven 325–350 degrees).

Check after 15 minutes; if fish flakes easily, it is done.

Garnish and serve with lemon or tartar sauce or melted butter or substitute.

Baked Northern (or other large fish) with Oyster Stuffing

Oyster dressing:

    1 cup oysters, chopped (not too finely)
    1 medium onion, chopped
    ½ cup celery, chopped
    2 cups seasoned croutons or bread pieces
    salt and pepper (use less if croutons are pre-seasoned)
    1 stick butter (¼ pound) or substitute, melted
    ¾ cup hot water

Sauté the chopped onion in the melted butter or substitute until translucent (about 3 or 4 minutes over low heat). Mix with other ingredients.

Scale northern and remove head, tail, fins, and draw. Wash thoroughly and rub inside and out with lemon wedge. Season lightly. Stuff northern and set upright on oven-proof dish. Brush outside of northern with Kitchen Bouquet and melted butter (in that order).

Bake in oven at 375 degrees for one hour or until large end of fish flakes easily.

If fish is not brown enough, brush again with Kitchen Bouquet. Brush with lemon-butter sauce before serving. (1/4 pound melted butter or substitute and 1 tablespoon lemon juice.)

Lemon-Stuffed Fish

4 fish fillets (1½ pounds each)

Ingredients:
½ cup celery, finely chopped
¼ cup onion, chopped
3 T butter or substitute
4 cups dry bread cubes or croutons
½ t grated lemon peel
4 t lemon juice
1 T parsley, snipped
1 T butter or substitute, melted

Place 2 fillets in a greased baking pan. Cook celery and onion in 3 tablespoons butter until crisp tender. Pour over bread. Add lemon peel and juice, parsley, 1/2 teaspoon salt, and a dash of pepper, and toss together. Spoon half the stuffing mixture on each fillet in the pan.

Top with remaining two pieces of fish, brush with 1 tablespoon melted butter. Sprinkle with salt (or substitute) and paprika and bake, covered at 350 for about 25 minutes.

Baked Fillets

Select two pounds of walleye or other freshwater fish fillets. Season with salt or substitute and pepper on both sides. Dip in milk or water and coat both sides with bread crumbs.

Place on a well-greased cookie sheet or in a shallow baking dish. Bake in a preheated medium oven (about 325 degrees) for about 40 minutes.

Meanwhile, prepare a solution of:
3 T lemon or lime juice
3 T melted butter or substitute

Spoon most of the liquid over the fillets after the fish has been in the oven about 5 minutes. About ten minutes later (15 minutes baking time), sprinkle the remainder of the lemon-butter mixture over the fish and shake paprika and parsley flakes over the fillets. Remove and serve after a total of about 40 minutes baking time or when the fillets flake easily.

Fillets Baked in Foil

Wash, dry, and season the fillets.

Lay each fillet on a separate foil sheet.

On each fillet place a generous pat of butter or substitute, a thick slice of onion, and a ring of green pepper.

Fold the foil over the fillet and seal.

Place the package in a preheated 350 degree oven for twenty minutes. (Thick fillets take a little longer.)

Serve with tartar sauce and/or lemon. You will enjoy a new taste experience that you will want to try again and again. You may also prepare fish in this manner for shore lunch—just bake them over coals.

Pickled Northern Pike*

Fillet the fish as you would a walleye—don't worry about the bones. Cut fish into small (herring-size) pieces. Wash.

Prepare a brine solution by adding one cup of salt of substitute (preferably pickling salt) to four cups of water. Cover the fish pieces with the brine solution and let stand overnight.

Step #2: Wash off the pieces of fish and soak in white vinegar three to four days.

Step #3: Drain, rinse, and place in jars (pint size is most convenient).

Prepare a pickling solution as follows:

To two cups of vinegar (if you like to use wine in cooking, use one cup of wine and one cup of vinegar) add:
1 onion, chopped (not finely chopped)
1 lemon, sliced
2 T mustard seed (level)
1¾ cup sugar substitute
4 bay leaves
dry mustard, one pinch
parsley flakes, one pinch
2 T olive oil or substitute
regular pepper

Pickled Northern Pike* continued

Put all in glass or crockery bowl. Stir twice daily. You may have to add more salt after it stands awhile. You can tell by taste. It's ready to eat after 24 hours. Keeps in refrigerator for one week. If you wish you can add more fish to mixture when fish gets low. Put in refrigerator and stir once in awhile so fish all gets under the liquid.

Courtesy Mrs. Donald Hester; Cass Lake, Minnesota